100 **words**

times

100 **poems**

equals

10,000 **sounds**

then

silence

100 **words**

times

100 **poems**

equals

10,000 **sounds**

then

silence

Norman Sinel

stonesthrowe press

stonesthrowe press
3721 Harrison St. N.W.,
Washington D.C. 20015
normansinel@yahoo.com

First Stonesthrowe Press edition January 2023

Library of Congress Control Number: 2022921376

Designed by Meghan Day Healey of Story Horse, LLC

ISBN 978-0-9993113-3-2

10   9   8   7   6   5   4   3   2   1

For Ellen
Family and Friends

One hundred words each poem
One hundred poems
Ten thousand words to fill the empty space of time
To fill the heart and mind
The heart grown hard
The mind grown stale
Can they be fixed by words by effort and thought
To see into the world
To make it
Simple
Can they be fixed by tomorrow's
Sunrise
Can the words bring them back
To life
Is it the thinking
The writing
Does the fresh sheet of paper
Call to birth a desire to live
To thrive for the first time free
Of shackles
Or is it the open window

› 100

The open window
Asks for my full attention
The light is the light
Of late afternoon in late fall
Not yet freezing
Most leaves fallen and raked
Some burnt orange and evergreen
Remain against soft blue
Full attention
An old concept
Do I stare
Do I hold my breath
Perhaps I let my eyes lose focus
To take it—the world—in wide angle
In it an angel I seek
A voice from the outside
To fill the inside
How full is full attention
What am I to gain
Will something new come to me
A spark from the air

A spark from the air
Started a fire in my stiff heart
Heat softened the knotted muscle
And I was moving slowly but
Moving
A strange feeling to step in my
Footsteps again and again but
Lighter
The exact steps
But each one new
Everything the same and not
The same
The same fresh sheets of paper
The same pen the same midnight blue ink
The same turning to old times
But not the same
A new opening
In the gray stone
Not a crack not a shaving
From its side
No
An opening in the stone
A true opening

> 300

A true opening
That is what we need
Each of us
Not a second or third chance
But a hole to swallow us
To surround us with open
An abstract concept to be sure
But virtually real
Real like the palm of my hand
The palm I present with my
Fingers spread ready
To receive the energy of the universe
Whatever it means now
I wonder whether that was
A different energy ten thousand
Years ago or whether
My palm would have been
Different
More willing
More willing to be part of
A larger space than
This small closed space

This small closed space
It is all that we know
We stand on tiptoe
To see over the ledge
We stretch our necks to
The fullest
There is no horizon beyond the wall
The mirror of our own
Boundaries reflect
Back on us
No slim breach to
Sneak through
No courage to make a
Crack
To shatter the image
To make a new view
To break through to a new being
No courage to become
A living battering ram
To splinter apart and to destroy the stasis
To open into a peacefulness
A peacefulness to sustain thought
Through bleak times

To sustain thought through
Bleak times
Is too common to need
Consideration by us
All times are bleak
Now
Pales by comparison with the past
And becomes the unformed beginning of a
Future that must be better
Or
There would be no reason to
Move into it
But there is the willingness
To force a kernel to pop
An openness to see
Luck and to embrace it
A humbleness to be soft
But not to break
For thoughts to be clear and new
For thoughts both old and new
Or
We are left
To stare into the dark with eyes glazed

To stare into the dark
With eyes glazed
Could be a great comfort
When the clarity of the sun
Is too much for the soul to own
The shield is temporary
And it will lift after
Four tides
Two high and two low
The surface film will melt into
A new day
That must be faced
Filled molded stacked
Upon the others until
The lean brings tension
As the inevitable
Tumble will lead to
The restart of the cycle
And a hope that
The new cycle will
Stretch past the hand's
Reach
Through the cloud cover
To deep blue space

Through the cloud cover
To deep blue space
Seems like a place to find rest
From a world
That is like shrapnel
To a soft spirit
A reason for the evolutionary growth
Of thick skin and numb nerve endings
A change that reaches some
But not all
Of us
And
Those denied
Adaptation's gifts are left to turn over cards
With no faces
To lose again and again
In a game with no
Rules to count by
Just collecting rectangles
With black numbers
That move them
Further and further
From any point that will make
Sense in the long run

Further from any point
That will make sense
In the long run
That is the direction
We are moving at a steady speed
Maybe even a per-second
Per-second speed
I know this in my soul
Even if my eye doesn't catch
The diminution
In size
The blurring of line
Or
The softening of color
Lighting a candle doesn't help
Nor does raising ones
Eyes and voice to the heavens
The direction is set
The flow of the river
Down from the hills
To the ocean
Splashing on boulders
Dropped by ice
Cracked by cold and lost
In the welcoming sea

Lost in the welcoming
Sea
I learned to breathe a different substance
And stretched out my arms
I moved my fingers
And
I risked opening my eyes
To a new world
One that was fluid
And silent
A great feeling of pleasure
Came over me
I was engulfed by it
I swayed with a gentleness
I had never known
I wondered if this feeling could
Last
Whether I could take it back with me
To the world of air
And direct sun
With my eyes wide
And my open mouth
I surfaced into a place
I knew would be different

> 1,000

A place I knew
Would be different
Was what I thought
I needed
Poets write about
What you need
And
What you want
A generation believes they are the same
Not mine
I was thinking
Survival not pleasure
But even survival has
Its many shades
With each of us picking the one that suits
What I thought I needed
I did
The path has been obscured
By the noise of
Ten thousand falling leaves
And
Ten thousand shadows
And
A red tail hawk
Circling over head
As awesome as the depths of night
And focused on the
Silent world below

Focusing on the silent world below
Will help shed the thoughts
That keep me
Out of the present
The number of tricks to avoid living are countless
The way to the present
Simple
But anything is simple if
You know how to do it
How to stop the abstract
How to stop looking forward
Or backward
How to plant your feet
On the ground below
How to set your eyes
On the don't walk sign
And
Take a quiet peaceful moment
While you wait for your turn
To step into the present
To take one more
Step in your journey

> 1,200

To take one more step
In your journey
You just have to pick up
Your right foot or your
Left
If that is what you prefer
You have to hold your head
High
But you must watch the ground as well
It would not do to trip
To break a hip and then
Spiral down to the end of the journey
Before the rest of you is
Ready to be done
You must take in the
Sun and the dark
The countless
Greens of the leaves
The color of stray flowers
And you must
Watch the path for
Hidden dangers

> 1,300

You must watch the path
For hidden dangers
A tree root covered by leaves
A copperhead resting in the shade
Just barely visible
But a harsh word from
Your traveling companion
Is a bite more cruel than
The sharp poisoned fangs
Of the beautiful
Diamond backed snake
There is no antidote
The words burrow deep
You smile and say
Your apology is accepted
Don't think anything of it
If there was an apology
You don't mean it
You don't know how to erase
The feeling that meanness lurks
At every corner
Your life is now
A careful walk with danger

> 1,400

Your life is now
A careful walk with danger
Maybe that is what life
Always has been
Maybe it's only with the
Movement of years
That danger
The dangers hidden around you
Come slowly into view
Maybe life is in no small part
Its dangers
So the walk must be walked
The pathway traveled with
Clarity and awareness
There is only one way
Forward and only
Memories of the scenery
As we move passed it
In haste or with deliberate
Mindfulness will survive
The joy and the fullness
Of it is grasped when
We look at where we are now

> 1,500

The joy and the fullness
Of it is grasped when we look
At where we are now
Not to look backwards
With regrets and
Not to yearn for an
Unknown future
Requires focus and commitment
Commitment to be
To be calm in the face of
The chaos and the swirling
Life with its
Second by second changes
That is a task for the
Fearless explorer
Only with the sharp
Focus of the now can
New thoughts be discovered
Only with the sharp
Focus of attention
Can our hearts fill to the brim
Fill to flowing over with light
Pure light

> 1,600

Filled to flowing over with light
Pure light
That is the state we long for
Even though we don't know
What it means
Is pure light
Peaceful
Is it quiet
Is it so bright
You close your eyes
Maybe it's just a concept
To over flow with pure light
Is to be filled with
Positive feelings
A sense that the life you live
And the world around you
Is beautiful
That the world is in harmony
And that harmony is good
Perhaps it is a sense
That life is a moment
Of unblemished joy
A soft breeze on your face

> 1,700

Life is a moment of unblemished
Joy
A soft breeze on your face
With deep blue sky
Set off by trees full of green
What more could there
Be in the moment
We could add a sound
Or two
A distant chain saw
A bobwhite
But no people
The road is packed dirt
Ruts on either side of
Stray grasses and tiny
White flowers
Poison Ivy on both sides of the road
So you must stay in the boundaries
It feels fine to walk and
To know you cannot stray
That it's not for always
It is only for now

> 1,800

You cannot stray
It's not for always
It is only for now
And now can feel like forever
If you have to color inside the lines
Of course
Wherever you color
It is between the lines
Maybe that is the thought
To keep dangled like the orange carrot
Enticing you to move forward
With goal driven intensity
The zigzag and the circle
The blob
They all fit into the journey
They all work their
Way into a scheme
A pattern for life's
Wonderment
Eyes open in awe
Hands ready for a new
Companion
That is definitely the way
To go

Hands ready for a new companion
That is definitely the way to go
With open eyes and
Arms outstretched
You must feel your way
To the next level
Intimacy has its rungs
To climb
Just like everything else
Each has its own key
And the rung you are on now
Somewhere in the middle of
The climb
Requires touch and intuition
You cannot know
So don't bother to look
It is not to be
Analyzed or parsed or pushed
Just feel with your fingers
Let them caress the
Would be lover
You will know
When it is the real thing

> 2,000

You will know
When it is the real thing
The air will be crisp
The sounds sharp
And the colors clear
Your breath will come in gulps
You will stand still
Struck by the pleasure
Of knowing
That at every turn
All life is before you now
That is what it is like
To be part of the
Real thing for the first time
That is a feeling
That usually comes only once
And that feeling
If it is a ten on the scale
And you really really
Experience it
Then after that be
Content with hoping for a nine

> 2,100

You must be content with hoping for a nine
A life full of tens would
Be too burdensome
You would carry your
Expectations like a heavy
Medallion around your neck
Before long you would be
Stooped over
It would be an effort
To see ahead
Or to look up to the sky
In wonder
And then you would
Become suspicious
You would clutch your burden
For fear that your best friend
Would take it
That is the burden
Of living your life with
Everything a ten
No
Walk tall
Cast off the heavy medallion
And let your eyes
Wander freely

> 2,200

Let your eyes wander freely
There is more to see by
Allowing the random
Than ever to be learned
By focus
The open road the open sky
A mouth needy to receive
That is where
Experience and wisdom blend
Easy to say easy to think
Hard to do
Where is the comfort in chance
The safety in tasting the unknown
It is all risk
High risk
Perhaps better to limit the chaos
Better to filter the unknown
So that the heart
Does not race
The skin does not tingle to a new touch
And
No stirrings upset
The straight line

> 2,300

No stirrings upset
The straight line
A person committed to a course
Must not waiver
With shoulders squared and
Head high
One walks with a deliberate step
Toward the goal
That was set
No matter that doubt
Wishes to intercede
Or fear desires a quick
Halt to the forward thrust
Not even bright green or amber
Eyes looking deep into your soul
Would let you
Stray from the narrow
There is a reason for walls
For lines of trees making a path
There is a reason for tracks in the snow
They are to lead us
Gently to our destination

> 2,400

They are to lead us
Gently to our destination
At least that is
What we were told
When we sat in rows
On hard wooden seats
Opening to the first blank
White page of our fresh
Back to school
Notebooks
With hard cardboard covers of mottled
Black and white
Eager is not a large enough word to capture
Our wide openness
This was our first chance
To enter a world so full
We could not put it into
Our bedside box
We could not contain it
In our arms
It was a world that expanded
Faster than we could dream

> 2,500

It was a world that expanded
Faster than I could dream
Every morning there were
New patterns of light on the floor
The bird song came in different intervals
And the jam filled
The holes in my muffin
In a way it never had before
That was just the beginning of
Sensory change
I had not yet had a thought
Heard a word
Touched another person
And felt whatever the
New connection was
Whatever the words
That would pass between us
Would be
The ritual had no repetition
The being in time was new
The being in time was exciting

> 2,600

The being in time was new
The being in time was exciting
Enough looking backward
Being caught in the circle of
What could have been
It is not possible to know
No
What you think might have
Altered your path might have
Smashed you into a brick wall
And planning for the future
Is no more fruitful
It is now that must be our
Focus
To break the chains of the
Puritan past
To take pleasure in what is
And to see beauty
Surrounding each step
Filling our eyes with
Dancing shadows
That is what is meant
By being alive

> 2,700

That is what is meant
By being alive
Feeling the new fall
Air on your face and hands
Watching a jet stream
Mark the deep cloudless blue
Tasting a tomato full of salt
Knowing that time is linear
At this point in our evolution
And not letting that hard fact
Take the joy from the present
That is what is meant by being alive
And that state of being is not
Easy to come by
It is much easier to
Drift into a state of absence
Than to open your being to the knowledge
That this is our only world

> 2,800

To open your being to the knowledge
That this is our only world
It should be a simple task
To see and accept this world
Do you have to sit perfectly still
Do you have to spin like a dervish
Or rise up in a balloon to see
The curve of our big blue ball
Maybe you just have to walk
Out your door
Maybe you just have to get your mail
Water a bush
Take out the trash
Maybe you just need to get out of bed
Kiss your mate if you have one
And sit down for breakfast

> 2,900

Kiss your mate if you have one
And sit down for breakfast
The day stretches before you
It's yours to live
Alone or not
You can drift
Come what may
As they say
Or
Choose with unwrinkled brow
Lunch with an old friend
A walk with an old lover
An hour or two with a soon to be
Lover
A walk alone until it is time
For dinner
And then an hour
With a pen and new thoughts
And tomorrow
After breakfast
If you are fortunate enough to be alive
You can look forward to the same
Range of choices

If you are fortunate enough to be alive
You can look forward to the same
Range of choices
Or you can change
Your patterned existence
Replace lunch with a walk in the park
Replace the walk with coffee
On a bench
A trip to the museum
Will set you into another century
You see the maid stir an
Old iron pot
As flames eat at the sides
And flush her face pink
You see the stray cat in the corner
Playing with its stunned prey
The trip into the past
Can set you on your way
Into the noonday sun

> 3,100

The trip into the past
Can set you on your way
Into the noonday sun
Which will warm your
Hands and face
Give you life on a late fall day
The orange and brown of
Leaves past their color
Sends a message that
Stirs the base string in your heart
Something you feel
Very faint
Very sad
Very real
You let the idea run its circles in you
Some trees are already bare
Others are full of brown
All are set off by a
Very deep blue
Your focus turns to the blue
And the crisp air and warm sun

> 3,200

Your focus turns to the blue
And the crisp air and warm sun
No need to dwell on
Linear time
No way to understand its
Rush
Counting leads to more counting and
Totaling
Which leads to subtracting
Eventually the number
Becomes zero
Zed
Nothing
And nothing makes no sense
Against a blue sky
Crisp air and warm sun
Counting is the forbidden fruit
It brings an awareness
An overwhelming sense of loss
That can shade the sun
Move blue into black
And make air thick
There is nothing to be gained
No lessons to be learned by
The counting reality

> 3,300

There is nothing to be gained
No lesson to be learned
By the counting reality
No
One must float
With no beginning and
No end
Grounded in the present
Filled with joy just for being able
To feel the warm sun
And
To hear the sound of a crow
And
To wonder what to make for dinner
And
Who to meet for coffee in the morning
Assuming of course
That you have another morning to drink coffee
And
To pick your donut
There are some
Who will make that same plan
And
Not wake to see the bright light
Of a new day

> 3,400

And not wake to see the bright light
Of a new day
Should be far off in the distance
It will occur
For you for me
For everyone
So it is not to be feared
Nor longed for
To take a phrase of now
It is what it is
Put it aside
And
Hold your head high
And
Walk the curving path
Go once around taking the forks
To the left
Then try it again taking the forks
To the right
Or just walk straight ahead
The roads all end at the same point
Full of brilliant light and sound

> 3,500

The roads all end at the same point
Full of brilliant light and sound
It was the sound that
Made me smile
There were dozens of melody lines
Layered around a deep roll of
Endless waves
The layers moved in and around each other
And lifted my spirits
I could feel the
Sounds on my skin
It was not quite the feel
Of a warm late spring day
But so close to it that I
Closed my eyes
And drifted into my teens
Not a care
My opening heart taking in the thoughts
Of the pleasures my
Young body needed

> 3,600

My opening heart
Taking in the thoughts
Of pleasures
My young body needed
Made my here and now self
Break into a smile
The feelings were bright
Against a backdrop with little color
The memory of the feelings was sharp
Not a stabbing sharp
Nor a note off key
But a snap
A crack that opened a stone that appeared
Solid and impenetrable
A smooth stone with a crystal lining
Surrounding its center
A fault line was exploited to become
A thing of beauty
Opened to the world
With purple and white shining in the light
For the first time

> 3,700

A thing of beauty
Opened to the world
With purple and white shining in the light
For the first time
The two halves lie side by side
In their own creation myth
Perfect specimens
Museum quality
Open for all to see
But only by chance
In its natural stone state
Its universe was closed
Silence was its world
As it thrived in darkness
Standing over the well lighted case
Wondering how it felt to be
Cracked open with the strike of a hammer
To become part of an infinitely
Larger universe
To be open to view
And to the elements

> 3,800

To become part of an infinitely
Larger universe
To be open to view
And to the elements
To have the rain wash
Your skin
Darkened from the sun
On a blue-sky day
Until thunder heads swept in with
The late afternoon
To laugh at the surprise
An act of random awakening
To embrace the magnitude
Of the massive dark that
Closed down the sun
Even if only for the time it took
To walk from the sea to the car
In that flash of time
The world changed
Its change back to blue was too late
A new page appeared

> 3,900

In that flash of time
The world changed
Its change back to blue was too late
A new page appeared
It wasn't blank
It was marked with the past
Some parts were colored in
Shades of gray
Others
The colors were brilliant
Half the page was ready to be filled
With the activities of this beginning
It was up to me to
Choose a color and
Select the pattern
It was up to me to
Fill in the page
Before turning it
To another and then another
No new page was empty
They all came with
Hints of the past

> 4,000

No new page was empty
They all came with
Hints of the past
Some were loud and
Controlling
Others soft and
Subtle
But each set the stage to
Limit freedom of action
Each came coded
A mystery to be unraveled and absorbed
A set of paths to keep the journey moving
Forward or at times sideways
Once a page was turned it stayed
Face down
There were no do overs
Awareness
If it came
Appeared in patterns on the next open page
The pages turned one after another
Building story upon story
Setting down its own
Unique highway to joy

The pages turned one after another
Building story upon story
Setting down its own
Unique highway to joy
Those who traveled with me
Had their own coded history
Dozens of highways piled each
On the other
All headed in the same direction
With different views from each surface
An illusory commonality
The structure seemed sound
But not the details
The world
Different for each traveler
To one the mountain was full of light and hope
To another it was mysterious
A height to be feared
To another it was
A reminder of a summer
From the time of youthful exuberance

> 4,200

A reminder of a summer
From the time of youthful exuberance
Is what we long for
Every step of the way
The lights should flash
When we meet someone
When we take in the first
Breath of outside air
On a new morning
When we touch the person
We love on the cheek
Or see the smile change the shape of the mouth
Or hear the opening measures of
An old standby
Hurling us back into a time
Past
Full of desire and dreams
Dreams yet unchallenged
Open arms of the future
That has passed and
Filled us with today

> 4,300

Open arms of the future that has passed
And filled us with today
And today
Is all but passed, as well.
It all blurs
A dense fog
Clouds covering and opening
The white/yellow moon
In an otherwise clear
Blue/black sky
Force a deep breath of wonder
For the float
And spin of this ball that holds us
Firmly planted in
The yesterday and today
A ball that spins us
Into a tomorrow we yearn to hold
Firmly
A tomorrow we know
Will bring us smiles and laughter
A tomorrow set in a stone
A rolling stone of
Memories of yesterday

> 4,400

A rolling stone of memories of yesterday
Bears down on us
With awesome speed
Weight to crush us flat
Pancake flat
Two dimensional flat
No time to say please
One more chance
One more chance
To make more memories
To soar off the spin
To look down at the
Rolling stone and wonder at its fullness
All round and gray
To see it run off into the distance
Growing small
Now just a dot so far
Below me
And to feel this day
Alive and gathering
Gathering the memories
For a new stone
Similar from a distance
Unique up close

> 4,500

A new stone
Similar from a distance
Unique up close
The dream myths of the living
Appearing to be common
Unique up close
Stripped of color
Not unlike the grand blue turning to gray
Ball receding at an awesome speed
A speed like light that flickers
No time to hold to something
Fast
It goes from our grasp
And it goes at a stunning speed
Yes
A stunning speed as the line of time
The thin as yet unbroken line
Of time
Of all we know
Smooths its edges to
Round
The unique dimming
The common taking hold
In quiet

> 4,600

The common taking hold in quiet
Frightens
At first
Then a calm begins to grow
As the colors turn inward
Turn from deep blue to
A blur of gray and back again
The colors growing inside
To fill a vessel once full
Growing to spill into the eyes
Into the smile
And then succumbing to
The drift
The drift that makes smooth
And gray the once so unique
The once so very special
The drift will
The same drift will bring
The crisp color back to the waiting
Calm
The color that will make the very
Concept of common
Unique

> 4,700

The color that will make the very
Concept of common
Unique
Has not been mixed
Has not been seen
May not exist
Except in the striving for space between
Friendship and loneliness
The tiny space between
Friendship and love
As eyes turn to lips and
Lips touch with the spark
Of the universe
A little shock that seeps into the soul
And once there grows and pulses
Sometimes like a hurricane and at others
There is a stillness that overwhelms
Leaving a silence
A silence of disbelief
That a hurricane can come and go
And come again
Fierce and steady

> 4,800

That a hurricane can come
And go and come again
Fierce and steady
Leaves us in a state of readiness
We can't let calm overtake
Us
We need to search for shelter
Not of straw or sticks
But of seriously crafted bricks
A shelter with few comforts
Only those needed for a life
Of the spirit
A life that moves in circles
Not in a straight line
We know that two straight lines
A set of tracks as the distance grows
Even when the whistle is still heard
Come together
They vanish into a point
That draws us to it

> 4,900

They vanish to a point that draws us to it
And as we come to see it close up
We long for the circle
Not the line
We long to move and think in clouds
Not certainties
We long to watch ourselves
Coming and going
Not just going
It doesn't seem a stretch
To lift ourselves off the
Tracks
Tied down on Christmas Eve
With the cow catcher ready
To push aside our brittle
Bones
And the black smoke
Filling the air with ash
The whistle coming
Closer and louder
As we close our eyes to
Dwell on the sounds

> 5,000

As we close our eyes to dwell on the sounds
We are overcome
Filled with relief
As the deep distant pulse
Of thunder rolls over the sea
Towards us
And white/yellow zagged lines
Move horizontally across gray
Water
We note the movement of the dark
Cloud
With an even darker outline
Relieved it may head north and leave us
Dry
The relief is mixed
A part of us wants the dark cloud to open
To force a change in our plans
To set us free
To make us laugh
While we count the seconds
Between the light and the sound

> 5,100

To make us laugh while we
Count the seconds between the light and the sound
That is what we were taught
One second equals a mile
The fire was not close
We would not be fried to a crisp in this storm
Knowing we were safe
As if there were any doubt
Made us giddy
We stripped down and walked back to the ocean
Sat in the sand and watched the darkness
Move away
Every second that gigantic dark cloud
Changed shape
Every second it was less of a threat
It was never really a threat
Just a mind game

> 5,200

It was never really a threat
Just a mind game
That was how we tried to
Play life
Just a fake here and a dodge there
Like grade school in the cement space
Outside the red brick
The ball was thrown at what seemed to be
Lightning speed
And we moved to the left to let it pass
And sometimes the right
Patiently waiting our turn
To win with a bullseye throw
Only one person standing was an
Early lesson
A lesson that set a barrier to compassion
A barrier to community
A barrier to a full and open life

> 5,300

A barrier to a full and open life
Does not have to be high
Does not have to be wide
Does not have to be strong
It is just something we feel
We can't touch it
And we can't pierce it by force
We can make it disappear
Just a thought
A touch
A smile
And it is down
Down for a time at least
It is not by effort or strength or fierceness
It is not by willpower or controlled
Living
It can be breached
An opening is there to be found
You must be open to the opening

> 5,400

You must be open to the opening
So you don't miss the rainbow of thoughts
Thoughts that can set in motion
A cascade of
Beginnings
So many to choose from
Hundreds of paths
Some straight others appear to
Loop back to the starting
Point
They all wave you forward
They all have a special appeal
You plant your feet firmly
Racing through you is the desire
To choose more than one
To stretch your arms and bring
As many of the soft paths
Together as you can hold in your arms
To become many and walk on all of them

> 5,500

To become many and walk on all of them
All the paths
To be more than one
To see from countless eyes
So there is no one narrow truth
So everything has a depth
A fullness that is new
To you
A fullness you are asked to explain
To guide others to it
To set down with instructions
Can you imagine
A manual to teach how to be
How to be open
Kind of makes you smile
Just to think of the absurdity
The absurdity of trying to teach
Open
Open heart
Open mind
Arms wide open to the universe

> 5,600

Arms wide open to the universe
Is that a little u or a big U
A little u and it's the universe of feelings
The universe of thought
A big U and it is a different matter
Mostly dark and vast
Just one more choice along the way
Maybe they roll into each other
You can't do the big U unless you first
Do the little u
That makes sense
How can you grasp light years
And black holes sucking everything into
Eternity
If you can't love
If you can't feel
If you can't choose to be everyone at once

> 5,700

If you can't choose to be everyone at once
At first
It is something you can develop
It starts with stones and flowers and trees
And moves to things that hop and run
And swim
And then to things that talk and smile
If you can learn not to treat the things
That talk and smile as a mirror
But as things separate from you
Maybe even not as things but as
Living beings
Free standing and separate
And if you really see all beings
As separate and free
From you
Then you can be everyone
You can be everything

> 5,800

You can be everything
Everything all at once
That is something to get
Your head around
Everything all at once
Will the weight of it
The volume
The noise of it
Drown you out
Or will you become so expanded
The Universe will seem containable
What a grand time you will have
Looking down at 10 quadrillion stars
Your eagle eye spotting planets with
Water
With life abundant
So many of them
Your sense of special and unique
Has drifted off past the boundaries
Of the expanding reality of the never ending
Universe
And there you are on the edge

And there you are on the edge
You are not afraid of falling
There is no place to fall
The edge and the middle are the same
Actually everything is the same
It is all inside you
You want to marvel at the feeling
The new feeling of oneness
But the feeling is so comfortable
It feels too right for special treatment
It just is as it is supposed to be
That is what you tell yourself
You wonder if these are feelings and thoughts
You can share
Would you get blank stares
Would your friends just nod and smile

> 6,000

Would your friends just nod and smile
Would anyone look into your eyes
And draw you to them for a hug and a kiss
Or would they look away
Embarrassed to see you open
Unprotected
Fearing that if you are like that
What will happen to them
Will they catch it
The openness
It could be a disaster
The walls are so well placed
So comfortable
Just a little crack and
Who knows
Tumbling down
A humpty dumpty event
And is there an inside
A very unsettling question
One with an answer
That will be clear enough
After the fall

> 6,100

After the fall
The light changed color
From a yellow orange
To a white yellow
Enough of a change to make me
Stop breathing
Just long enough to adjust
The world had changed
My world had changed and
I assumed that meant all the world
Had changed
The sounds were softer
The breeze more gentle
My friends came to me
Looked me in the eyes
And wrapped their arms around me
They tilted my head up and
Kissed me
We were all connected
Connect by a fine thread
From each other to the Universe
Expanding with it
We all smiled

> 6,200

Expanding with it
We all smiled
The ride had begun
The stretch of hills and brambles
Gave way to the entrance
The cleared pathway
To the stars
If not the stars
To the feeling of stars
Tiny points of light sprinkled above
Each asking us to join it
Our hands outstretched
Faces full of laughter
We raised our arms to the dark blue-black
The vastness dotted with an expanding
Array of dazzle
We looked back to each other
Full now
Full of a wonder and joy
We were ready to move on
To take the steps we needed
To take

> 6,300

To take the steps we needed to take
Required no thought
Instinct moved us
We assumed forward
It could have been sideways
Or maybe even backwards
But to us it was movement
Guided by the divine
And that was enough
Enough to get us started
The key was not to look for the end
Not to look for the structure
The key was to move
With the invisible current
To move at a calm pace
To look
To listen
To expand into our surroundings
To be alive
To color in the gray
And to give life to everything
We touch

> 6,400

To give life to everything we touch
Should not be a challenge
It requires very little
Just an open heart
The willingness to be present
Not looking ahead
Not looking behind
Not looking at all
Just being
No beginning or end
Grounded in the joy of it all
The feel of the air
The heat from a body
The sound of a laugh
Or sigh
It really is easy
Yes
The most elusive and difficult thing
Is quite simple
A letting go
An embrace
A soft sound
A strong touch
That is what it takes
To expand into the whole

> 6,500

To expand into the whole
Is not without danger
The line between whole
And breaking into a million
Pieces
Is not visible
One opens up blind and
Hopes to reach the perfect state
To get as close to it
As is safe
Safe is to be cherished
If it does not set false
Boundaries
It is the boundaries that stop us
The boundaries hold us together
And they are the constraints
Holding us back
The struggle is constant
It is silent
How we deal with the struggle
Defines us
Closed or open
Willing or unwilling
To be and to grow

> 6,600

To be and to grow
To repeat and repeat
Does it help to hear the same
Message
Over and over again
Or does it just make it harder
To follow
To be
What does that really mean
If we sit
If we stand
Or walk
Does that mean we are present
Are we open and aware of every
Sound
Each color
The countless shades of green along
The forest path
Are we tuned in to the clouds
Pushing each other for space
In the blue
Can we just sit
Just be still
Our thoughts weaving a tapestry
Of illusive imagery

> 6,700

Our thoughts weaving a tapestry of illusive imagery
We hold out our hand to touch
First it is a unicorn
Then a mountain lion
Then the statute of a bull
Then soft colors blending into
Each other
Bring a quiet
A quiet that slows breathing
That slows seeing
That brings us to a point
On a circle
It could be a point placed anywhere on
The circle
To be is to be content with
The placement
Not to yearn for
Further up or down
Or around
And most important
Not to yearn to be in it
Or outside of it

> 6,800

Not to yearn to be in it
Or outside of it
Means you work towards
Peace
Not inertia
One is full
The other empty
With peace comes change
Growth seeks those
Not striving for it
That is a state of being
Hard to come by
Hard in our culture
A culture of merit and greed
A culture of judgment
And placement
Placement on the scale of success
A culture of winners and losers
Ours is not a culture that
Celebrates grace or luck
Or the fullness of a person
Ours is a culture of angst
It seeps into our bones

> 6,900

Ours is a culture of angst
It seeps into our bones
And tries to hold us
In place
No movement is the currency
Of angst
The circle tightens
The walls come up and
We are deep in the dark of the
Silo
Reasonably comfortable
At first
Then a little less so
Then claustrophobia
Sets in
And now the angst
Made up at first
Now it is real and understandable
Who could feel alive
Who could feel open
At the bottom of a silo
Maybe someone with dark glasses
Or someone single focused on
Winning
But not someone who is real

> 7,000

But not someone who is real
An odd turn of phrase
We are all real
That is what this tour is about
In our own way
We are real
The issue is we have no clue
What real means
Eat
Sleep
Love
Produce
Reproduce
Ponder
Those all seem real
And they are real to the person in the
Silo overwhelmed with angst
Just like they are real to the person who
Has climbed out of the silo
And who has put angst aside
That person stretches toward the deep blue
In the sky
Opens up
To breathe in the world

> 7,100

To breathe in the world
Should not be too much to ask
The question may be
Who is asking it of us
Or
What is asking it of us
If it is some automatic nerve firing
Fine
Just keep it firing
If it is some higher order
Great
Listen to it and follow
It
Follow it to the ends of the earth
Or even to the end of the Universe
Which has no end
So that is difficult
To achieve
But it keeps you moving
And it is the state of not moving
That turns you back into the circle

> 7,200

And it is the state of not moving
That turns you back into a circle
Has you chasing your tail
Has you wondering why
Why are you staring into space
Why are you at loose ends
Why are you shrinking
It takes effort to break the circle
And that comes in the form of no effort
It will make sense when the motion returns
You will know you are moving when the
Trees flash by
When the spring breeze turns to snow
When the cicadas come back from their sleep
You will know you are moving
Because you are moving

> 7,300

Because you are moving
Your lungs fill with clean air
Your hair flies behind you
Wings grow on your ankles
Because you are moving
Your soul fills with joy
Your mind expands into a
Million directions
Which turns out to be
A good thing
If you had thought about it
You would have thought it
Would have been a bad thing
But no
The million thoughts
Played with each other
Wove themselves into
Grand patterns
And then settled into a peaceful whole
And that peacefulness settled
Into your body
And softened your face into a smile
Your soul into brilliance

> 7,400

Your soul into brilliance
Was new to you
The light was everywhere
There was no glare
No discomfort
There was a sense of well being
Knowing you were where you
Were supposed to be
Even if the feeling
Is fleeting
It is worth the experience
An experience to stay with you
And to guide you
Even when it has passed
To encourage you to
Seek the light wherever
And whenever you can
It is always there
Waiting for you
It is quite vast
And can wait patiently
For you and for everyone else
Who wishes to seek
Its healing powers

> 7,500

Its healing powers
Fill the Universe
And cannot be diminished
They are elusive to most
Not by design
By the subtleness of its
Power
Few realize they are surrounded by a force
That heals
That creates joy
That requires nothing in return
A force that can be harnessed
Only for good
Such a benign power
Is unique
Something so powerful
Freely available without condition
Is not intuitive
It is not something that we see
Every day as we walk down the street
We cannot see it embedded in the trees or
In the color of the clouds or the sky

> 7,600

We cannot see it embedded in the trees or
In the color of the clouds or the sky
It is not hiding
It is there in plain sight
For all to use
To heal and find joy
Inexplicable how few see this light
How few believe it exists
And how few wish to explore
What does and what does not
Exist
And how many would be frightened
To know this freely available
Healing energy just sits there
For the taking
Just sits there and waits to be
Called
It does not demand ritual
Or loud cries
It does not demand

It does not demand
It does not ask for connection
It just is
It is there for each of us
Alone or guided by someone
Who feels it and sees it and knows
How to ask it for help
Help for someone who needs help
And that might be
All of us
We all may need to have a chance
To be with the all being light
To let it embrace us
To let it fill us with a spirit
Of open
A spirit to move us one step closer
To wholeness
No matter how whole
There is another level

> 7,800

No matter how whole
There is always another level
Of whole to wash over us
If we let it happen
And each level yields
The chance for another
Until we are part of the
Light in the clouds and the sky
Figuratively
We are part of that light
While fully alive
Fully engaged in our
Day to day
Lives
This is not hard
And it is not secret
It just requires an openness
To the world
A willingness to embrace
The unknown
A willingness to put aside
Fear
Fear of being
A whole person
Full to the brim
With joy

> 7,900

A whole person full to the brim with joy
That is what each of us should wish
To be
And it is so simple
There is no five-step plan
No twelve step effort
It is no more complicated
Than watching a puffy white
Cloud against the deep blue
Of a July sky
At the ocean
Standing at water edge
With a 180-degree view of the horizon
And the vastness of the ocean and sky
Stretched out before you
That is what can fill you to the brim
There is no thought making
Your brain whir like a mid-century fan

› 8,000

There is no thought making
Your brain whir like a mid-century fan
There is just you and the sand
And the ocean and the sky
And a little white cloud or two
Shape changers
With no boundaries
It is not the only way to
Fill with joy
But it is a good way
Quite a respectable way
Another is to wait for the end of day
And wonder at the color
The subtle color that each cloud layer takes
As the sun falls further below
The steady line that separates the sea
From the land
Until the color is gone

> 8,100

Until the color is gone
We should commit to joy
That is not a major commitment
It is quite easy and natural
It is like opening your eyes
In the morning
There you are
Somewhere between sleep and
Non-sleep
Your body is quiet and comfortable
And the room is filled with silence
And warmth
The covers are just the right
Amount of heavy
And your mind begins to develop
A cadence
Now will
Will take you
On the road to the new day
Once you open your eyes
You are awake
You are now out there in the bright world

> 8,200

You are now out there in the bright world
It is not a take it or leave it thing
Like it or not
You are in it
And now that you know how to
Fill to the brim
You open to the day
Your senses taught
Your feelings ready
To happen
That is what it is like to be
Out there in the bright world
You don't have to leave your porch
You can just stand there and wait
For the heat of the summer day
To take you in
To wrap you in the
Weight of the warm air

> 8,300

To wrap you in the
Weight of the warm air
A feeling that comes a
Few dozen days a year
Different from the chill
Of a sunny winter day
The blue is similar
But the sun is white not
Yellow
And the air is moist
It would fill you with
Terror if you could not
Just turn around and go
Back into the warmth
A space surrounded by walls
Filled with heat from an
Enameled cast iron stove
Snuggled into the corner
Surrounded by gray stones
That will not burn
Even as the stove glistens
With heat
Fed with oak

> 8,400

Even as the stove glistens
With heat
Fed with oak
And an old coffee pot
Sits on the flat top
Staying warm
Maybe hot
You wonder if you
Should dress in wool
And walk the back forty
That is what they did
In the good old days
They put on wool
And walked the back forty
To see whether the fence needed mending
Or to just catch a glimpse
Of hawk
Hoping its next meal
Would hop out from behind the bush
That is how simple life is
A little peak out from behind the bush
And then endless darkness

> 8,500

A little peak out from behind the bush
And then endless darkness
And so life goes for the creature
Unknowing
The end
Right around the corner
That was sobering as I
Strolled through the crunchy
Thin layer of ice on the once
Tall grass
With a smile in the knowledge
That soon enough the
Grasses will straighten
And turn green
Even with that thought
Front and center
Another slid in like a voice over
Tomorrow is promised to no one
A simple line delivered in a simple voice
In a forgettable movie
And I still try to live by it

> 8,600

And I still try to live by it
A concept of now
Not tomorrow
Like the comment from a neighbor
Over a fence heavy with grapes
Plan to live forever
He said
And
Be prepared to die tomorrow
That too stuck with me
Even though they are not the same
Plan to live forever is not the same
As
Tomorrow is promised to no one
And be prepared to die tomorrow
Also is not the same
I can live with the confusion
It is an opening of the heart
To live
Between these concepts
To focus on here
And now

> 8,700

To focus on the here and now
Is a little worn
Maybe a lot worn
Maybe
Worn out
Maybe it is not just here and now
That is worn out
Maybe focus is also not what it is
Cracked up to be
Maybe focus is a narrowing
Squinting to see a bird on a branch
And not seeing a thousand
Fly by in formation
Maybe focus is linear
At a time when we need to be
Peripheral
We need to see and take in the
Full spectrum of color
And sound and feeling
Maybe that is not what focus brings

> 8,800

Maybe that is not what focus brings
An openness to color and sight and sound
And ideas and laughter
Maybe focus is a trick
A trick pushed on us by greed
By some inherent need to succeed
To win
A necessary attribute to be on top
To honor the straight and narrow
To hone the skills of the worker beings
Not to provide a full rewarding life to those
Who strive
Who are super-focused
They are too near sighted to help
They cannot see the needs
Of those closest to them
Or see their own needs
To act on them

> 8,900

To act on them
Their own needs
Would require an awareness
That could only come when the sharp focus
Blurs into a view of a vast world
One with clouds and blue skies
With trees of so many shapes and sizes
They rival stars in our efforts at counting
One with sounds heard and silences
Magnified
By their depth
That is what can be in store
For you
If you can lose your focus
Counterintuitive
Not what has made this
Mad land so great
As the winners like to say
Take a chance
Turn your back on that
Controlling gestalt

> 9,000

Turn your back on that controlling gestalt
Winning may not be what it seems
And in the long run it separates us
To win is to cause someone else
To lose
And the loser does not forget
Who has taken their spirit
And left them a hollower soul
Then what have you won
You are walking tall among a crowd
Of broken beings
Where is the joy in that
Soon there will be no place for you
No place to turn
The loneliness will be overwhelming
Perhaps if you acknowledge
It was mostly luck
Perhaps then it would
Be ok

Perhaps then it would be ok
Luck is a leveler
It brings in the randomness
Of nature
It makes one humble
You did not do it all on your own
You worked hard
You seized opportunity when it
Presented itself
But that is not the whole story
The whole story has a lot to back fill
You were born in a family that was not
Broken
You were of a skin color
Your country found acceptable
You lived on the right side of the tracks
And you did not get hit by
An eighteen-wheeler
And you went to summer camp

> 9,200

You went to summer camp
Your house was full of books
And newspapers and magazines
That was all part of the luck of the draw
You took the left fork
The right would have led to the jungle
And disaster
It is okay to be happy with what you have achieved
It is not okay to think you did it
On your own
Nothing is done
On your own
There is always a sliver of something else
Sometimes it is bigger than a sliver
Sometimes it is the spoon we use as a baby
Silver for some
Gold for others

Silver for some
Gold for others
Plastic for the masses
If they have anything to eat
Be proud
Be thankful
There is more random than you think
Random lightning strikes
Random good fortune
Random sink holes
You managed to come out on top
That is good
Good for you
Neutral to others
Neutral unless you can harness your good fortune
To help others
Which would be their stroke of luck
You can be an instrument of luck
That could be great fun
Behind the scenes fun
No one would suspect
You
You with a quiet face
You are their luck

You with a quiet face
You are their luck
The amount of luck circling the universe
Is infinite
You can share freely
If you are a luck magnet
You can spread the wealth
If you just had some random luck
You can still spread what you have
That is what luck demands
An open heart
A willingness to share
No envy
A true joy in the joy of others
A belief that we all share a common
Thread
One that binds us
Whether we know it or like it
That is the only way we can survive
With abundant spirit

The only way we can survive with abundant spirit
Is to know there are ten thousand ways
That is how we must see the world
How we must see others
How we must see ourselves
We are ten thousand in one
And we can see the one in the
Ten thousand strands of others
We can feel the common strands
And know that is the way to the future
To know and feel the connection
To know and feel that we thrive
If we are together
And we fail as a lone unit
Believing it is only us
That counts

> 9,600

Believing it is only us that counts
Only us that deserves a giant share of everything
That is how the end has begun
And it has begun
It is well on its way
Picking up speed as we
Stumble
Little cries from here and there
Too soft to be heard
Too many words that no longer have meaning
A sense of community that exists in
A few
A few with no means to influence
No way to talk without the noise
Drowning out their message
Change
Change how we live
Change how we think
Or there will be no we

> 9,700

Change how we think or there will be no we
That is not an over-the-top thought
That is our reality
Even the most open
The most caring
The most optimistic
Know
Know behind all the curtains they hang
They know the real end game
They know there is nothing that can
Stop the process
The process of splintering
Of turning one against another
The process of giving the planet
To the little flying things
Which might be just fine
There is no reason to hold on to
The top of the pyramid
King of the mountain
Ends with a fall

> 9,800

King of the mountain ends with a fall
That is not news
We have known that since we were young
If the bigger kids did not
Pull us down
Then the big pile of dirt
Slid from under our feet
There was no way to stay
King of the mountain for a whole afternoon
No way to last an hour on that
Sandy peak
We should not be surprised
When we feel the wind in our face
As we hurtle down from the top
Towards a bottomless
Pit of disaster
That sounds very dramatic
It will not be so obvious

> 9,900

It will not be so obvious
It will just be one thing after another
That makes our nights
Sleepless
At times we will think
We have made it easier for some
To survive
We might even think we have made it possible for some
To thrive
We will hold on to the little things
We will believe they are important
But
Once we open our eyes
Once we see
We will see the downward spiral
Of this thing that stands erect
We will sit with crossed legs
We will watch the clouds with
A new silence
The silence of knowing

> 10,000

About the Author

Norman Sinel grew up in New Haven, Connecticut. He received a BA in English from Yale and a law degree from Stanford. He was the Senior Vice President and General Counsel of the Public Broadcasting Service (PBS) and then spent the rest of his lawyering career as a Partner at Arnold & Porter. He lives in Washington, D.C. and Truro, Massachusetts with his wife, Ellen, who is an artist.

CPSIA information can be obtained
at www.ICGtesting.com
Printed in the USA
BVHW030424140123
656250BV00008BA/41/J